OUT OF
DELMARVA

Cover design and layout
Hartley-Wildman
and Michael Carmean

All photographs by Cary Kamarat

for Nicole

Acknowledgements

My sincerest appreciation and thanks to new friends on the Shore—the Art League and Writers of Ocean City, Maryland, Management and Staff of the Worcester County Library, Karen McClure, Gina Ashton, Seth Merson, Bob Schaller, Rina Thaler, Katie Rosinski, and Ruth Alcorn—and to old and future friends on both sides of the Bay.

OUT OF
DELMARVA

By

CARY KAMARAT

Hartley-Wildman Publishing
2015

Library of Congress Control Number: 2015956281

Photography and text copyright
© 2015 by **Cary Kamarat**.

Published in the United States by Hartley-Wildman Publishing, first printing by DC Library Press, Washington DC.

ISBN: 978-1-63273-009-1

CONTENTS

DREDGER

BEHEMOTH

Behemoth waiting in the sand,
heart of iron and bold creation,
dredges depths for humankind
lost in dreams of renovation.

Between the known and unknown strands
an ocean swells of cold perception,
but sacrificial barriers wend
along bright shores of warm redemption.

THE NOR'EASTER

We were happy sailors, chasing
darker waters—pushed eight knots
to a mounting bow wave, romping home
across the Bay, we swept the wind
wild and heeling, heading up,
to a northerly gust.

The Nor'easter circled round to pound us,
shook some sense into clouds and nightfire,
storming waves of salt-brewed menace
swallowed a waxing moon—enough
to wash us all far out to sea,
if it had a mind.

As if tired of sinking ships
and dashing dolphin pride, it came
to dwell along the tortured lane
where each tumbling wave that rises
dark, and born to bully and spite,
gives no rest.

On shore, you opened arms to catch
the breakers coming in like holiday
pirates, caps of foam and black
knives slicing the moon's delight,
and we made passage through the cut,
just under the wire.

But while you shuttered home and hearth,
and mind, against the tempest bearing
down on boards and fears, we came
ashore and thanked our lucky stars for refuge
harboring life and limb—and let the Nor'easter
clear our minds, for another day.

WINDOWS ON THE BAY

SHIPS AND STARS

The cruiser beamed its masthead light
moored to a solid horizon, bright
as a jealous planet at war with the Goddess Star.
Bedecked sublime in blacks and grays,
parading past the end of days,
(when ships and stars turn stocks and bonds
to brightly colored children's games)
both star and planet held fast as night,
bound to the end of Orion's kite,
sailing past the dust and fire of a rarely Milky Way.

Then without so much as a *mind-if-I-do*,
Orion stepped into our living room,
with that vaudevillian flourish of his all over the glass,
with a *Hatcha! I got a million of 'em!*
and stars and planets aligned above him
(where chorus lines of constellations
dipped and tucked—ya gotta love 'em),
would've stayed there doing it all night too
if Mom hadn't started, *Just look at you!*
You can pick up your burning gasses, and get outa my milky way!

So, that fiery hunter spent the night
ascending, leaving us far behind
and trying to forget the Goddess far below—
But he looked so dashing in belt and sword,
a downright dandy and a proper lord,
that we knew we'd all have trouble letting him go,
because once you've seen his nibs perform
you'll never do what you thought you might
as social reformer or socialite—
you'll just have to do your schoolyard best
to get a grip on *Réalité*.

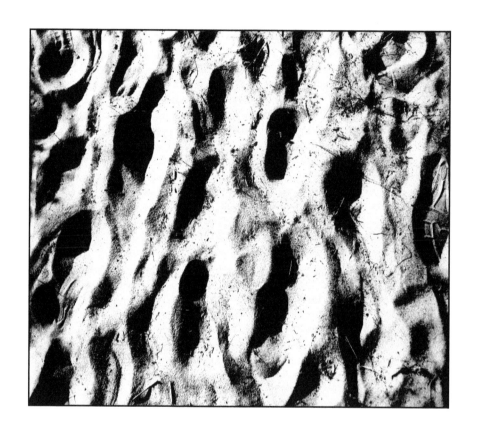

RUSH HOUR

QUESTIONS

Was the beach too vast and daunting,
when he pulled himself ashore
pounding on the icy sand,
strong arms, determined flippers—
Was the seashore vast or welcoming,
when he left the sea?

Did the frozen foam along the tidemark
rasp the wound that drove him out,
to a safer place in another world,
from sea to land and fear to promise—
Did he feel the promise?

Did he know he'd been a favorite morsel
for the sabre tooth of a darkly fathomed shark
that tore a crimson gash across the waist
that sickened sleek along the fur now,
discolored pink along the tear now,
blackening at the center of the pain—
Could he bear the pain?

And the giant that was man,
who came along the shore to help
and carry him to a healing place,
with towering shields, strong baffleboards
that trapped him in the caging space, and spoke
in a mild caress of the naming voice,
in an old tradition of the manly kind,
and whistled softer tones that closed
his eyes in peaceful rest—
Could he feel how much the giant loved?

SAMMY

IN MEMORIAM

Down at the water's edge, the memories rolling home
where wind-driven sands wed one place to another,
I hold on to past and future lives beckoning
to lowering skies that crowd the sea,
beached whales come to rest
on shores of pale devotion.

I remember her now,
always at this time recall
the scraggly bits and treasures
of our brushed lives— passion, joy,
the rage and laughter in our aging eyes,
those aging eyes that taught me love and color.

I sing an ancient hymn forgetting
half the rhyme once learned by rote,
a benediction for youthful days shared,
and now the bridge and candle between our sundered
moments along this bountiful path
of grace and time.

A CONVENTION OF GEESE

Across the cold-woven heart of the bay,
Smoothly burdened with an offer of frost,
A convention of geese gather thoughts of the day,
Sorting hopes and devotions for the next Pentecost.

Faces fixed to the selfsame cardinal point,
They daydream of grassy slopes framing the dawn,
Bidding all wintry mixes *Begone and aroint!*
As some of them laugh, and some of them yawn.

No minutes to approve, no budget to chart,
No ganders and geese beating wildly to wind;
There's a settling air, in a universe apart,
Albeit a loud one all shrilling and dinned.

Hunkered down in the glow, with avian finesse,
Mates a-twitter and fussing in shadow and gold,
Very few have convened under pain of duress,
Most seem happy to huddle, in the God-awful cold.

WINTERVIEW

SYMMETRY ON A WINTER PIER

SKYWARD

I stand here at land's end,
eyes follow the streaming pier
to the heart of a watery world.

Then legs spring vast and free
in time with the cantering hound,
over tired wood, broken shells,

used barbs and bits of tangled line
that complicate our flight
to the soul of time.

He runs ahead, gets there first
and points to a yearning
somewhere just beyond,

where a lone heron commands the marsh
morning fresh, brush-painted wings,
neck outstretched to show the way

to another infinity—
Rising.
Skyward.

OLD DOG

He spends his days, now, dreaming of past glory,
of lanes and other paths that he has known—
his mastery of each trail-blazing foray
relived, each road well-labeled as his own.

He's seen himself as Heaven's Bold Protector,
and still would, if he'd waken to the task.
But body and mind each sails a lonely vector—
the one must soar; the other can only bask.

From time to time he lives a joy remembered
in every furry fiber of his Self—
he comes to greet, and share his burning ember,
to teach the simple path from wags to wealth.

CATCHING THE LIGHT

CATS AT THE GOLD COAST MALL

cat mother bask in yellowlight
watch the man in healing glow
cover the kittens in loving eyes—
snuggle thanks. then cry and go.

watch the woman mother night
leave the food and fidget slow
feel the goodness warm inside—
stalk to thank. then snuggle and go.

walk the building shadow pool
ocean scent of shells and fish
man and woman lift the spoon
toss the morsel from the dish—
cry to thank. stalk and go.

poise to bask in silverlight
moon in joy and smiling now
time to scamper laughing flight—
stretch to thank. then cry. then go.

PLAYBOYS

DUNE BABY

WHEN A BEAGLE GOES SHOPPING

When a beagle goes shopping it's never a chore;
there are tidbits and gambits and wonders galore
that can make him forget what he came out for—
when a beagle goes shopping, it's bliss.

When this hound makes the rounds of the marketplace,
he starts praying he'll end up flat out on his face
in a spilled pile of kibble, or a sugar disgrace—
when a hound makes the rounds, it's like this:

he'll go trotting along from glimmer to gleam,
unaware that there's nothing that's quite as it seems:
he'll nuzzle the *cat*nip and tug at *bird*seed
and try jackets that *never* would fit.

Then he'll snap to the scent of a chicken-y whiff
from a holy mound stacked on a heavenly skiff,
at the back of the store where no one's admitted
but careless as Christmas, he's in,

inspecting the stock for a tear in a bag,
walking up to just anyone, diva or hag,
inquiring as to *Who might be currently tagging
the rejects for discount?   ...or gift?*

When a beagle goes shopping there's so much to buy—
every parcel and morsel that catches the eye
and the nose and the paws and the jaws gently prising
the life out of Dad's money clip.

31

JUST BECAUSE I WANNA

When you reach that age called *ripe*,
you may run a sailor's risk of turning *a wee bit ornery*.
It's not so much a matter of lashing out
in *pagan despair*—
or telling preschoolers stories with markedly
unhappy endings—or even joining the family Christmas
for the sole purpose of ending the evening
in a *bar room brawl*—No. It's more.
It's that inveterate and unsettling need to have things
just the way you wanna.

I once had a television. It had old filmz *noirz*,
and new filmz *technicouleurz*, and the original
ethnocentric sitcoms from the Garden of Eden,
and saccharine-sweet commercials
you could sing along with friends—
because idiocy was never subliminal,
and only rarely tried to teach *Robotnewthink*,
Brush-a brush-a brush-a, get the new Ipana,
mm-mm good—
and you could always turn the frickin-thang off,
if Mommy taught you how to,
because it was on free airwaves
it was uh-huh it was, but then—

they captured the waves and made you pay
for cramming them through cables,
and handed you a packet of
televised manure—

five hundred versions of the same five channels:
      fifth-grade game shows,
      low-overhead talent shows,
      a variety of reports on impending Armageddon,
      the usual sitcoms (from the Garden of Eden)
      and talk talk talk shows talk talk talkin,
but only one film *technicouleur,*
because if you wanted more filmz *technicouleurz*
you had to buy the Cable Barons
one more yacht, one more island,
one more ticket to the new-slave trade-show.

But I've been feeling kind of *ripe,*
and just a *wee bit ornery—*
So I went and threw my television on the tallest
scrap heap I could find.
sang a sweet *Jamaican Farewell.* And now,

I just watch my microwave
heatin up my coffee, poppin up my popcorn—
because one:
it's not nearly as demeaning,
and two:
just because I wanna.

THE BRIDGE

When the need for silence
supplants all other needs,
for a silence that builds
mountains out of mists,
there's a bridge
like a child's painting of itself,
a simple thing in whites and blues
that comes to life
and laughs across a pond,
halfway between a twinkle and a nod—
I go there for the journey
and to ask, and learn,
why children play.

CHESAPEAKE

Thermals rise above the salty bay,
across five carriage lanes five miles
of cantilevered arches spanning
white capped swells, and winging gulls
that need to teach how it's done.

Lay fears down on the terror shore,
and laugh at the ferryman who'll drive
your car, to keep your teeth from chattering
shattering all those holiday dreams,
you're free to soar while jackals run.

Where there is burden overarching care,
allow this flight-born path to take you
where souls restore that feast on air,
and riding thermals charm the Fates,
then face the east—where yarns are spun.

BEACH TORII

PATTERNS

Symmetry of form and soul,
patterns of contentment,
heron trails that cross a quilted sky—

Mist-born jasmine
fills this clapboard frame
with gods and lovers—

And a sorcery of horizons
turns a simple cottage
to a golden-turreted palace—

standing firm
against invasion.

BEACH TOWER

SIGNALS

THE TERROR

Tenderly the light descending
candles turning
woven strands
her upturned hands to hold the flow
a mother's tears.

She lit the flame
remembering morning songs
when children played
on blue-rimmed beaches
of a dream,
their casting pails
and castles bravely holding
back the tide
relentless tide
relentless time, until

Hearts were Frayed against the Cutting Edge
Another Cause Another Slaughter
Burning Dawn when Suns Descending
Burst the Dream to Fiery Shreds

that light these candles now.

She never thought a healing flame
might one day hope to mend the sun,
and bring the children
home to stay.

SUN JOURNEY

THE WAY HOME

Power lines still
rise and fall the way they
did when we were tiny huddled in
the back seat ruddy-nosed and watching
father's huge and powerful hands on the guiding wheel.
Raining kindly down along the caring glass
light-woven and wind-pressed they
tumble, droplets falling to
a timely end.

ANOTHER SPACE

Time after time,
between the outward journey
and the coming home,
strewn flowers cast
malingering shadows
that stretch and drain
the moments left
to a silent ebb.

Truths we wanted to tell
belong to another space,
to other days and lies
in tomorrow's house.

If there were only one—
one truth, one house,
one time and space—
we might pretend,
along with puppies, kittens,
other innocents,
that we have mastered every moment
of this mortality of ours.

TOWERING PINE

Towering pine, apart and lonely
on a path to the waking forest,
autumn's broadleaf splashes
fallen blown across its shadow,
like remains of last night's bright balloons
left scattered on the party floor.
Far below its green cap wisped and brushed
into the sky, it whispers statuesque,
commanding accolades.
Its eloquence approaches now as I draw near
and we both lean into the freshening breeze.

I touch its lingering slumber,
and majesty disturbed flows deeply,
life-current trembling with its tales
and silent billows that gather me up,
beseeching—don't ask me how I know—
in need
of a soft embrace.

                    And so I do.
                    And then I see it—
                    in my mind's eye, a rumbling car,
                    with bumper sticker shrinking
                    down the road:
                            TREE HUGGER…
                            TREE HUGGER…
                            TREE HUGGER…
                            TREE HUGGER…

HERITAGE

QUEEN MARY'S SEAT
ON CATHKIN BRAES
for the St. Andrew's Society

Along the rising cinder path
on the rich and green, as the mizzle falls,
and bluebells hide their color swaths
and magpies strut to a dancer's call:
—*Are you askin'?* —*Ay.* —*Then I'm dancin'.* Say,
can you feel the turbine slice the wind,
like a sky-flower spinning its hope and prayer?
But neither was granted the fallen queen
whose spirit sits upon the cairn.

From where she watched in darkened grace,
Queen of Scots in an ancient wood,
her kindred, cast in battle array
in a sea of guns and pikes and blood,
swept moor and village at Langside Hill. Then,
ambush turned to rout and chase,
till the Regent halted a sacrifice
of the Queen's thousands, as they bore the shame
of a failed assault, and a fateful flight.

I have had to sleep upon the ground
and drink sour milk—the Queen would tell—
and have been these nights like the owls...
—and embroidered secrets in a tearful vale.

She declared herself free of her land's miseries,
when the time came to lay her white neck on the block
'twixt the martyr's red robe
    and the beheader's black work.
And her cowering lapdog,
    and the hundreds who watched,
were drenched in the blood of the dead queen's skirts.

SHADOWBIRD

AN EERIE LOSS

Julie Christie was in a movie,
a long long time ago.
They changed her blood to a synthetic ooze,
and left her adrift in an almost human state,
of all things.

With certain cravings she really shouldn't have had,
she held a swatch of blanket
like a laundered baby-banky,
pressed it to her cheek with a sensuous rub,
gazing high and wistfully through a neighbor's window,
beneath the dust blown trees of a post-pluvial,
no longer merry, Old England.

"They're not like us," she said, to no one in particular,
"They're not like us," she repeated,
"no one wants to be unpopular."
She caressed her banky, again and again,
in case we missed it, the first few times.

And Ms. Jane Doe was in a commercial,
not very long ago.
They changed her phone to a Cybernetic Panel
she'd sorely miss, if she lost her Contact Slate,
of all things.

With certain needs she thought she'd always had,
she held it out before her
for all the world to see
like a swatch of baby-banky on TV,
gazing deep and wistfully through the TV window,
in a dust-blown studio of a post-constitutional,
no longer Yankee-Rebel, America.

"If you're like me," she said, to everyone in particular,
"If you're like me," she repeated,
"no one wants to be out of touch."
And her eyes caressed her Cybernetic Panel,
again and again, in case we missed it, the first few times.

CYBER-TIME

CINEMA UNBEARABLE

for František Vlàčil

Guests around the wedding table,
Men in sackcloth, women in veils,
Smile and glance from bride to groom,
Bride—too young to wed a father,
Groom—too fatherly to wed.
Eyes avert; the Son approaches
Shameful, timid, hesitant.

He loves this bride, this girl his age
Peeking over veils at youth
Like her own, in quiet lust.
He brings a gift to his new mother,
Brings a basket to his love,
Places it gingerly on the table
Where the guests afford him space,

Well within the virgin's reach,
Soft beneath his mother's breast.
And she delves into the basket,
Freeing fragrant petals, tossing
Bits of laughing flowers skyward,
Till they turn to bats and vermin—
Till the guests depart, undone.

FOUR FACES
for the Chabad of Eastern Shore

Four faces in the photograph,
sepia-tinged and lost in time,
passed along the cousins now,
token words of grief—

Faces chiseled dark and distant,
untempered in the melting pot,
this is how they must have looked
the day they left Judea.

This is Sarah, our grandmother,
sister Sarah and the children—
Boys are boys, but this one must have
been a blessing (mischicvous mouse).

And these lines above the mouth,
this one could've been a doctor,
lawyer, politician, lover,
maybe more—or maybe not.

But the girl. There's something lost
inside those eyes. How can they shine so,
in this dark and faded photo?
Bright and dark—and hardly gone.

Surely there's the loss we cling to,
for Grandmother and the children,
we who never even knew them—
now that death camps have been cleaned.

TRANSUBSTANTIATION

MISS KITTEN AT BLUES ALLEY
for Eartha Kitt

Down the alley, where jazz lovers
find a *reason* for the blues,
down Blues Alley, in the faux-glow
of gaslight gone electric,
pools of whiteness spill
over all the hues of red brick
holding up the night,
above a shopfront quaint, but hot—
promising Something Big
for that lovin' Georgetown crowd.

Step lively 'cross the tiles,
and wet your whistle just a bit,
then find a table meant for *two*
where *four* lovers squeeze to please
and there she is—she's on the menu,
between that Sarah Vaughan Filet
and *Bugnon's Ginger-Mango Brie*
it's Miss Kitten's Catfish Po' Boy,
sweet and brown, served all crispy—
'leven-fifty, what a deal.

Down the alley, where jazz lovers
find a *seasoning* for the blues,
down Blues Alley, there's a boudoir
high above the café noise.
On those wide and wobbly stairs,
where stars descend then fly to rest,
sits Miss Kitten, scared as always

steppin' out on that icy stage.
But she can warm it to a hot pink.
And she knows it. So she stands,

pushes off then purrs and snuggles
down the steps all time-worn
quiet as a hidden past,
in a cloud of French perfume.
Here comes Miss Kitten—someone whispers—
she likes million-dollar daddies.
Someone said she found one too,
that's because there IS a God.
Now the memories ebb and flood,
voices hush, round the room:

From plantation to Manhattan,
to the White House, London, Paris,
Kitten stepped out of *her* alley
long ago, paid her way.
So she rises to the stage now,
where the hangin' spotlights sizzle,
looks across a padded shoulder,
lets a Cheshire smile just beam
through that midnight lamé sparkle,
under Cleopatra eyes.

You know she'll laugh out loud,
if she catches you in love and wanting more—
that's when it really begins to flow and spin,
around that cabaret floor
at Blues Alley, for that lovin' Georgetown crowd.

HAIKU

Girl beneath the dust
rescued from the circling fires,
challenging the sun.

Golden in her grief,
a sanctity of ravens
cloud the loving glance.

Life and trains derail,
still she'll travel far and wide
in her children's eyes.

HIGH COUP

The polls will say exactly
what they've been designed to say,
emerging paradigms grow stale
on the dancing floor—
an old familiar ploy,
with Latin American flair,
but without the maracas,
and salsa-drenched for the party.

Still the nation is free, in spite of itself,
and just to be sure I'm voting
for Senator Alabaster Gleam,
for he is clearly the more
cosmetically appropriate choice.

PHANTOM

HOWLS

For Sebastià Serrano

In the beginning was the Voice,
And then the Word.
And Song then wed them both
To breath, and so became
Inseparable from life.

But howls must intercede.
For heavens howl
And know the tongues of beasts
Beloved or not, tempered
Or distempered, they must howl.

Once for the mist that learns to rain,
Once for love and once for grief,
Once for lofty schemes and places,
Once for the joy of one's own passing,
And once at last, as from the first,
for pleading's sake.

From first to last of every life,
Voice and Word
And Song awaken,
Until divine oblivion's voice—
Life's reverse and mirrored image—

Howls.

COAXING THE KITE

CYBER-YOGI
A Modern Tale with Ancient Roots

Cyber-Yogi went to market to buy a kite,
for dancing,
for he knew just how and where to catch
a kite-tail in his teeth.
With a hearty megabyte he'd soar,
and heavenly prance on the wings of a dance
to leave his wish at heaven's door—
though no one really knows for sure
where the door of heaven starts—
but it's lovely bright and easy to spot
from a dancing kite so,
Cyber-Yogi went to market to buy a kite,
for dancing.

On all sides there were pits and falls,
and body traps graffitied walls
with splattered acclaim for sundry roads
that could take your name and twist it,
till you never knew who you were,
or what,
or when.

He saw a tree that suited his kind,
a human tree with soulful roots,
and between them hidden doors were jammed.
If you got them open you could tumble through
like Alice falling deep and deeper,
mysteries rising all around—

but some of the doors you could coax ajar
to steal a peak at Forevermore
(Just think.)
(But no.)—
Cyber-Yogi was going to market to buy a kite,
for dancing.

He saw the Panic Merchants then
selling tales to souls they'd bought,
deathly tales, both night and day,
they'd stew folks in their own dismay
till everyone was overwrought.
And smiling, they'd report the news:
"Hurricanes and Tidal Blues
with No. Earthly. Solution."
(Just think.)
(But no.)—
Cyber-Yogi had come to market to buy a kite,
for dancing.

At long last dodging all temptation,
badgering devils and bad vibrations,
he came to the crest of Old Kite Hill,
best spot at the fair for spotting
thrilling deities and such.
He paid his dime for a climbing kite,
and with the power of a child who's quick to love
he rose and soared with all his might,

and soon had everyone, young and old,
looking up to where he hovered
megabytten to the tail of a dancing kite.

And watch they did, as long as they dared,
stretching, reaching up,
straining to join him
high, above the dance.

HOME AT DAWN

ABOUT THE AUTHOR

Cary Kamarat, a native of Chicago and graduate of Northwestern University's School of Communication, has taught at Evergreen State College in Washington State and NATO Defense College in Rome. His educational research has been published by the *Academic Exchange Quarterly,* and his poetry has appeared in *The Federal Poet, Poets on the Fringe, Prospectus: A Literary Offering,* and the *District Lines Anthology.* It has also been published online at *First People: Native American Poems and Prayers,* and *Israel National Radio.* His photography has appeared in *The Tulane Review* and *District Lines,* and he has reached a broad international audience through his travel blog at *www.travelwalk.blogspot.com.* His debut collection *Travelwalk: Poems and Images* is available at Amazon.com. Now a resident of Maryland's Eastern Shore, where he takes a sailor's delight in the beauty of the Chesapeake, he continues to read his own poetry at several venues in the Washington DC area, in Chicago, and on the Eastern Shore.

Lightning Source UK Ltd.
Milton Keynes UK
UKHW022216240122
397636UK00007B/365